Both Sides Win!

3 Secrets for Success in Customer Negotiation

Logan Loomis

BOTH SIDES WIN!

———◆———

3 Secrets for Success
in Customer Negotiation

In memory of and appreciation
for Bob Wolff—the best negotiator
I've ever known—and to Alyce.

Author's Note to the Third Edition

In 2002 I wrote this little book to highlight some key practices for negotiating when you are faced with a need to negotiate great return *and* great relationship at the same time—customer negotiation. Negotiation is such an integral part of business success that I thought clients would benefit from a practical primer on key success factors in negotiation—something that you could throw into the briefcase and use as a quick reminder on how to stay on your game and achieve your goals. The response to this little book has been more enthusiastic, frankly, than I expected. So here we are with a third edition.

One of the great joys this book has given me, personally, comes from people sharing their "ah-ha" moments—the moments when they used a practice in the book and got an outcome that made them want to continue the practice. There is such enthusiasm in people's voices when they share with me, for instance, that it turned out that what they initially thought the problem was, wasn't really the problem at all. It always takes me back to my ah-ha moment when I first used the listening practice outlined in this book. I can remember it like it was yesterday, but it was 1990.

I was the CEO of a natural gas trading and marketing company. I had just been to a leadership training program where I was instructed in the active listening process—the rephrasing and reflecting process—that I discuss in this book. To be candid, I hadn't used it—that is until Chris, the VP of Sales, came into my office at 6:00 one evening. He blurted out, "If I have to work with Charles, I'm out of here!"

We knew Charles was going to be difficult to work with when we hired him—and he had lived up to his press. Chris and I had agreed, however, that Charles had trading knowledge that made dealing with his difficult personality extremely worthwhile. Chris really needed to work with Charles to gain important trading knowledge. My first instinct was to go into persuasion mode: to remind Chris that we knew Charles was difficult when we hired him and to encourage Chris to stick with it. I didn't, however, follow that first instinct. For some reason, the amount of money that I had invested in the leadership program popped into my mind and, in a split second, I decided to actively listen to Chris rather than try to persuade him to stick it out. To my surprise, I quickly found out that the real issue was different from what I initially thought.

I simply responded to Chris by saying, "You seem upset Chris." Chris shot back, "You're darn right I'm upset. Charles treats me like I'm five years old." I thought, what does that mean? I said, "He doesn't respect you?" Chris clarified, "No, it's not that he doesn't respect me. He just doesn't seem to get that I'm catching on." As I continued with the process, what emerged as the real problem was that Chris had come way up on the learning curve and was ready to take off the training wheels. With that knowledge—knowing the real problem—Chris and I had a productive conversation about how to realign the working relationship. He didn't need to stop working with Charles; he needed to work with Charles differently.

We got a good solution—to the real problem—and his intense emotion was diffused almost instantly! That was my ah-ha moment. As I sat in my office after Chris left, I said to myself, "This is amazing. I have to get good at this!" That commitment has been a great benefit to me in negotiations—and really every facet of my life. I sincerely hope that it has the same benefit for you as you use the practice.

As with the second edition, I have taken the opportunity in this third edition to share a few additional insights throughout. As you read this little book I encourage you to apply the practices broadly in your daily interactions with others. The introduction that follows begins with the observation that negotiation is the basic way we gain what we need and want from another person. Another way to say this is that "negotiation" is a basic or essential human process. We do it naturally—every day. Through the negotiation training program that I deliver, I have discovered that there is a common tendency to think of "negotiation" narrowly as something you only do when you are involved in a commercial transaction.

3 Secrets for Success in Customer Negotiation

When people have the epiphany that these practices also work in their "personal" lives, I know they get it. They get that negotiation is a life skill. It is my hope that the insights shared in this little book will help you achieve success whenever and whatever you negotiate!

Sincerely,

Logan Loomis

New Orleans, Louisiana

March 8, 2012

Both Sides Win

Introduction

WHAT IS THE first thing that comes to mind when you hear the word "*negotiation*"? When I ask that question in workshops I hear answers like compromise, win, conflict, risk and haggle. Many people think of negotiation solely in the context of a transaction, deal or dispute. In reality, negotiation is something we all do multiple times every day—and we can do it without unnecessary compromise and conflict.

Something as simple as selecting a restaurant for lunch can be a negotiation. For instance, you and your friend—let's call him Jim—agree that you want to have lunch together. You want Chinese; Jim wants

Italian. You're actually about to enter into a negotiation with Jim because you differ on what kind of food you want. You have some shared interests: you are both hungry and you both want to have lunch together. But you also have some differences: Italian food versus Chinese food. The process you go through to agree on a restaurant is a negotiation.

Imagine that you and Jim are from my hometown of New Orleans. You remember that both of you are interested in trying a new restaurant; you've heard it serves great crawfish etouffee. You suggest that restaurant as an alternative to an Italian or Chinese restaurant. Jim thinks it's a terrific alternative. A winning solution—you both win because the crawfish etouffee turns out to be delicious.

The point here is that negotiation is fundamentally the back-and-forth communication we use to reach agreement when we have some interests that are shared and some interests that are different. One of the most challenging kinds of negotiation is

3 Secrets for Success in Customer Negotiation

negotiating with a current or prospective customer with whom you want to have a profitable and lasting business relationship. Why is customer negotiation challenging? Because you have to negotiate both great return and great relationship at the same time. Just like your lunch with Jim, you and a customer—or prospective customer—will likely have some interests that are shared and some interests that are different. Customer negotiation is how you identify and handle the differences to achieve a profitable outcome.

There are three practices that, over the years, have been my secrets for success in customer negotiations:

1. Get Curious.
2. Know your value.
3. Understand your power—and theirs.

They have been secrets to success for me because they have helped me build relationship, gain influence, handle upsets, benefit from sources of power that many people tend to give away and, importantly, avoid getting sucked into price discussions too soon.

This book will explore each of these practices. My goal with this book is provide a primer on customer negotiation—a *brief* discussion of these practices. Something that you can throw into a brief case and pull out to quickly refresh your perspective on how to best approach a negotiation with a customer—or anyone else.

I am dedicating this book to my late uncle, Robert Wolff. Uncle Bob was the best negotiator I have ever known. He was a very successful oil and gas landman. He could negotiate leases where others had failed. He helped me get through college working for him. A lot of what I will share with you in this book I learned from Uncle Bob during those summers in the early 1970s. One thing he taught me is: if you really look for it, there is generally a way to achieve mutual gain rather than mere compromise— you can achieve an outcome where both sides can win. That's why I've titled this book *Both Sides Win!* My career in law and business has validated what Uncle Bob taught me about mutual gain. It's certainly not always achievable; but in my experience it has been achievable more often than not when I follow the practices outlined in this book.

The following pages summarize each of these practices. I hope that they help you achieve higher returns and build long-lasting relationships with your customers.

BOTH SIDES WIN

Practice 1: Get Curious

NEGOTIATIONS ALMOST ALWAYS start with a statement of positions. "Positions" are what customers' say they want, what they say they will do and what they say they won't do. You also start every negation with your position on what you want, will do and won't do. I received some very valuable advice about positions when I was negotiating labor contracts with union representatives. The advice: never take an initial position as gospel. There is an old Zen saying that gives insight into the perils of negotiating at the level of positions:

*Problems seldom exist on the level
at which they are expressed.*

19

Both Sides Win

———— ◆ ————

Positions are only one dimension of what is actually going on. You might think of a position as the surface level of the negotiation. You need to get below the surface to the deeper interests that underlie any position to improve both your relationship with the customer and your return. Our interests—our underlying needs, wants, concerns, troubles, pains and fears—are the real drivers of behavior. Our position is a stance we decide to take; our interests are the reasons why we decide to take that stance.

Key point: only view a position as a starting point.

Master negotiators don't get locked into negotiating over positions. **Instead, they get curious.** As famed 20th Century financier and presidential advisor Bernard Baruch said, "Millions saw the apple fall, but Newton asked why." Master negotiators develop a curiosity mindset: they wonder why something is important or why someone is taking a particular position. They know what the customer is saying; they get curious about what the customer is not saying. They ask themselves: "What interests are underlying that position?" "What caused them to take that position?"

A negotiation about vacuum cleaners illustrates the value of curiosity. The head of housekeeping of a high-profile, high-end hotel told the General Manager that housekeeping wanted new vacuums. Replacing vacuums in a hotel is a sizeable expense. The General Manager immediately started into a lengthy discussion about the type of equipment that was needed. It finally occurred to her to ask, "Now, why exactly do we need new vacuums?" To the GM's surprise, the answer was that the hotel had gotten new computers for everyone, so housekeeping felt that they were entitled to new vacuums. Truly, problems seldom exist on the level at which they are expressed.

It was not about vacuums at all; it was about needing to feel valued and appreciated. The GM came up with a very satisfactory way to meet the underlying need—the real need—without buying new vacuums. Both sides won.

This outcome illustrates the importance of curiosity. The General Manager would not have addressed the real underlying problem had she not paused to get curious regarding why they needed the vacuums—and she would also have spent considerable money on new vacuums.

Her first reaction was, however, to launch into problem-solving mode. She is not alone. I have had the pleasure of training now literally hundreds of people in the practices outlined in this book. As a result I have identified a pervasive tendency toward *premature problem-solving*. It may be an epidemic in American business. When someone states a problem or objection there is an instant reaction to shift into problem-solving mode or into persuading. That shift is, however, premature. You first need to make sure that you understand the real problem.

3 Secrets for Success in Customer Negotiation

Regardless of your effectiveness as a problem-solver or persuader, you are ineffective if you are addressing the wrong problem or only a part of the problem. Pause before you start problem-solving or persuading to make sure that you have answered a critically important problem-solving question: why do they want that?

Mastering the ability to pause is actually a tremendous source of power in a negotiation—and in life generally! In the press of life today, we seem to be more and more conditioned to react or give quick answers rather than considered responses. Because learning to engage the power of pause has been so helpful to the people that I've worked with since this book was first published, I am giving it more in-depth consideration in this third edition. My colleague and friend, Nance Guilmartin, has written a valuable book on the power of pause, *The Power of Pause, How to Be More Effective in a Demanding, 24/7 World*.[1] I will share some of her keen insights later in this book.

Developing a curiosity mindset can both diminish the tendency toward premature problem-solving and expand your options. As Mark Twain says in *A Connecticut Yankee in King Arthur's Court*: "She was wise, subtle, and knew more than one way to skin a cat."[2] I encourage you to think of a party's position as only one way to satisfy an underlying interest—one way to skin a cat. Once you understand the interests that caused the customer to take that position in the first place, you are able to explore other ways to satisfy those interests; ways that might be both acceptable to the customer and more profitable or more acceptable to you.

Reconciling positions is the most common approach to a negotiation even though it limits your options. This is how it works. I take a position. You then take a position. We then each make concessions until we have agreement. Basically, we meet somewhere in the middle. Although concessions may be necessary at times in a negotiation, I like to avoid that path as much as possible. There is a better way. Try to reconcile needs and interests before you make concessions. To illustrate, let's talk about pizza.

You and your friend, Jim, are hungry again. Jim says, "Will you share a small cheese pizza with me?" You are on board for pizza, but you would like to share a large pepperoni pizza rather than a small cheese pizza. If you take the approach of compromising your positions, you may end up with a medium cheese pizza: Jim makes a concession on size and you make a concession on toppings. If you first explore interests, however, you will likely create better options—different ways to skin the cat.

So why does Jim want a small cheese pizza? Not very hungry? Doesn't like available toppings? Limited funds? You decide to get curious regarding why Jim wants a small cheese pizza. You discover that he is on a tight budget this week. Once you understand that constraint, you can begin to reconcile your interest in a large pepperoni pizza with Jim's immediate budget constraint. One option might be for you to buy the pepperoni pizza this week if Jim agrees to buy a pepperoni pizza for the two of you next week. You both win: you both get pepperoni pizza within Jim's budget!

This agreement is possible because you have both shared interests and different interests, as is usually the case. You share an interest in a large pepperoni pizza. Jim's interest in economy this week, however, exceeds his interest in size and toppings. You, by contrast, are more interested in size and toppings than the cash outlay this week. The path to a mutually satisfactory agreement lies in reconciling your different interests in immediate cash outlay. There are multiple ways to reconcile that particular interest. You have options—more than one way to skin that cat.

I know from experience that I gain strength in a negotiation when I tap into the other party's underlying interests. By tapping into why they have taken a position, I have an opportunity to go beyond the limits of that initial position and propose new options; options that create the maximum mutual gain. I may not have to compromise if I get curious. We all might enjoy that large pepperoni pizza!

> **Key point:** Avoid premature problem-solving. Pause and get curious about why someone is taking a position; get curious about underlying needs and interests.

Influence: Additional Payoff for Curiosity

You also increase your influence when you are able to tap into the other party's underlying interests. Influence is a currency of power in both the immediate negotiation and the ongoing relationship with the customer. We all want to gain the ability to influence a "yes," but gaining influence is one of life's paradoxes. You really don't gain much influence by stating and arguing for your position. **The paradox is that you can gain more influence by listening than you can by speaking!** Let's take a look at why and how:

- Why does listening create more influence than speaking?
- How can we listen in a way that builds influence?

Why does listening create more influence than speaking?

By listening effectively you increase understanding and rapport. Understanding and rapport are keys to gaining influence. Why? It has to do with our human nature.

We all want to be understood. Psychologists tell us that our need for understanding is second only to our need for food and shelter. To thrive, we all need to be understood—to be listened to. When people feel that you understand them, you have satisfied one of their deepest human needs. That, in turn, opens up their willingness to listen to and understand you. You have tapped into a powerful and fundamental principle of influence: reciprocity.

3 Secrets for Success in Customer Negotiation

Reciprocity is one of the most compelling methods of influence. Some of the best research on the rule of reciprocity specifically, and influence generally, has been done by Robert Cialdini, Ph.D. He presents his research in his iconic book *Influence Science and Practice*.[3]

The rule of reciprocity simply states that we should repay in kind what we receive from someone—we should reciprocate. Cialdini's research indicates that all human societies subscribe to the rule of reciprocity.[4] Why? Because ingraining the tendency to reciprocate is good for society; it's good for all of us. Cialdini explains it this way:

> A widely shared and strongly held feeling of future obligation made an enormous difference in human social evolution because it meant one person could give something (for example, food, energy, care) to another with the confidence that the gift was not being lost. For the

first time in evolutionary history, one individual could give away any of a variety of resources without actually giving them away. The result was the lowering of the natural inhibitions against transactions that must be *begun* by one person's providing personal resources to another.[5]

So the impact of the rule of reciprocity is that when you give something tangible (e.g., food) or provide a service to someone, you are actually creating an unspoken, but nonetheless very real, obligation to return the favor—to reciprocate. As Cialdini notes, "We will go to great lengths to avoid being considered a moocher, ingrate, or freeloader."

This principle of reciprocity also governs situations of a purely interpersonal nature; for instance, giving *understanding*. When you give me understanding—something that I find valuable on a deep personal level—I have a natural compulsion to reciprocate. I have a natural compulsion to try to understand you.

3 Secrets for Success in Customer Negotiation

For example, I got a call a number of years ago from one of two feuding partners in a professional services firm asking me to facilitate dialogue between the two of them. He said, "You're the only one he'll listen to." No magic there. I had consistently made a conscious effort to listen to and understand his partner; his partner was reciprocating when he listened to me. I was happy that I was able to get the two of them talking—and listening—to each other again.

The willingness to listen to you and to trust you doesn't begin with the customer. It begins with you. People decide to listen to you—or *not* listen to you—based on your actions. It is paradoxical that it is in the silence of listening during a negotiation that you gain influence. By first genuinely listening to and understanding someone, you are able to establish the foundation for mutual understanding that is so critical to a long-lasting commercial relationship. Reciprocal understanding creates a sound and sustainable foundation for mutual gain.

Both Sides Win

———— ◆ ————

Key point: We all want to be understood. Psychologists tell us that our need for understanding is second only to our need for food and shelter. When you give understanding, you are actually gaining influence because you are tapping into the influence principle of reciprocity. The rule of reciprocity simply states that we should repay in kind what we receive from someone—we should reciprocate. If you make an effort to understand me, I have an unconscious obligation to reciprocate and try to understand you.

Before exploring how to listen in a way that creates influence, let's take a look at another impact of the influence principle of reciprocity: there is an inclination to make a concession to someone who has made a concession to you. Reciprocity is the force that compels us to reconcile our positions. If I make a concession in your favor—I come off of my position—then you feel an unconscious obligation to make a concession in my favor. That's why as a seller you have an instinct to start high and as a buyer you have an instinct to start low. You want to give yourself room to make concessions. You want to give yourself room to negotiate.

You improve your potential for gain if you explore the interests that are driving the other person's position *before* you make a concession. First, get all the interests that you can on the table. You may actually find that you can satisfy a need or interest without cost to yourself: you can make a concession that has value to the other party but doesn't cost you anything to concede.

For example, you may be negotiating a transaction to buy a parcel of real estate and the purchase agreement includes a standard close date 60 days out. You discover that the seller is interested in closing within 30 days. You are indifferent. Even though you are not giving away anything you value by agreeing to a 30-day close, by making a concession on the close date (which is valuable to the seller) you are creating the potential for the seller to make a concession in your favor on something that you do value. In short, starting high or low is not the only way to give yourself room to make concessions. You may discover some unexpected concessions that you can make with great gain if you surface needs and interests *before* you make concessions.

Bottom line: there is value in listening before you concede. The following section shows you how to listen in a way that builds influence.

How to Listen in a Way that Creates Influence

The following three-step process will help you connect in a way that allows you to surface the other party's underlying needs and interests:

1. Listen: show up and get in sync.

2. Confirm understanding: pause, shift, and check in.

3 Secrets for Success in Customer Negotiation

———◆———

3.   Manage reactions.

Negotiators who have mastered these steps have a huge advantage. Let's take a look at what is involved in each step.

Listen—Skillfully

Listening is a process. By doing it skillfully, you surface underlying interests and position yourself for better outcomes in a negotiation. Doing it skillfully begins with your intent. To listen skillfully, start with the intent to understand underlying interests; start with the intent to get curious. You can tee up the opportunity to get curious by asking an open-ended question like: "Why is that important to you?" Or, "What are the consequences to you of getting that result?" When the customer responds, go into full-receive mode. How? First, show up!

All of us have the tendency to listen with the intent to respond. In your head you might be saying to yourself, "What am I going to say when he or she stops talking?" For instance, do you ever catch yourself in a conversation where you're "just listening" but your mind is full of chatter? During a negotiation, for instance, while the other party is talking you might be thinking about how to position your service or respond to concerns or objections. You're not really listening; rather, you're preparing to talk. Most of us naturally focus on what *we* think or feel about what is being said—how *we* see it. While we appear to be silently listening, we're actually having our own internal conversation. We start problem-solving, figuring out what we'll say, judging or reacting almost as soon as the person starts talking. Our internal conversation distracts us; we can't really hear. We are there physically, but we don't really *show up* for the conversation. We can only listen effectively if we are not talking or preparing to talk—if we fully show up for the conversation.

I was recently doing some sales coaching with a Vice President of Sales for one of my clients. As we explored why his closing ratios were off, it became clear to him that he was not showing up. He was not really getting curious about the prospective customer's' underlying needs and interest. He was too focused on thinking about what he wanted to achieve and not focused enough on really hearing the needs and interests of the customer. His close ratios instantly improved when he started showing up. In his efforts to remind himself to show up—to quiet the internal conversation and focus on the customer—he would tell himself to "clear the mechanism." "Clear the mechanism" is from the film *For the Love of the Game* starring Kevin Costner.

Kevin Costner portrays Billy Chapel, a veteran major league pitcher at the twilight of his career. He is trying to prove to himself and others that he still has what it takes to be successful. At one point in the movie, you are aware of what Billy hears from the pitcher's mound. You hear all of the sounds in the stadium—the taunting fans, people blowing horns, the passing subway—and can realize how hard it would be to concentrate. The movie then lets us inside this pro's head. The noise fades to silence as Billy says to himself, "Clear the mechanism." His full attention is then focused on the batter. Clear the mechanism is Billy's way of clearing his mind and focusing. It worked as effectively for my client as it worked for Billy. In a sales call he would remind himself to clear the mechanism—silence his internal conversation—and focus on the customer.

When you show up for the conversation, you remove the distractions of your internal conversations. You commit your focus on to the customer. You don't listen with the intent to respond or persuade; you listen with the intent to understand.

Key point: Show up! Listen with the intent to understand. Silence your internal conversation so that you can focus on understanding the customer's needs and interests. Clear the mechanism.

Get in Sync

You might think that when you're not saying anything—when you are silent—that you are not

3 Secrets for Success in Customer Negotiation

communicating. If that's what you think, you are dead wrong. In your silence you are actually communicating very powerfully. A significant part of communication is transmitted through non-verbal communication like tone of voice and body language (such as facial expression, gestures or movement).

Part of listening effectively is to get *in sync* non-verbally by establishing non-verbal rapport. One way you can establish non-verbal rapport is by creating a common physiology. It's a process in Neuro-Linguistic Programming (NLP) called "mirroring" or "matching." A basic mirror is simply to copy the other person's position and movement. If the speaker, for instance, is sitting forward, then you sit forward. If the speaker is sitting back, then you sit back. For the other person, it's like looking in a mirror. We all mirror each other naturally when we are in rapport—it's one of our ordinary human instincts.

Participants in my negotiation workshops enter this natural state of rapport when I get them deeply engaged in sharing a meaningful story. I suddenly ask them to freeze! I then show them that they are sitting in mirror images of each other.

6

They have entered the natural state of rapport. It happens unconsciously for all of us when we are really engaged. To build immediate rapport in a customer negotiation, however, I encourage you to do it consciously. Make the conscious decision to sit the way the other person is sitting.

Rapport is the ability to step into another person's shoes—to make the person feel that you

3 Secrets for Success in Customer Negotiation

understand him or her. Getting in sync with the person's physiology—merely sitting the way the person is sitting—is a great way to step into that person's shoes. Words work on a person's conscious level; physiology works on an unconscious level.

By building rapport—getting in sync non-verbally—you are tapping into another fundamental influence principle: liking. It rarely comes as a blinding flash out of the blue that as human beings we are obviously more inclined to say "yes" to someone we like; someone who is similar to us. If you are mirrored physiologically—simply sitting like the other person is sitting—the other person is unconsciously thinking that you are like him or her and therefore must be alright. Once that happens, the influence principle of liking kicks in and rapport develops. Mirroring creates physiological rapport and evokes the influence principle of liking. Again, words work on a person's conscious mind, but physiology works on the unconscious.

Both Sides Win

---◆---

Key point: Mirroring someone—simply sitting like the person is sitting—helps create quick rapport. Mirroring builds influence because you tap into the influence principle of liking.

Consciously mirroring may appear to be a manipulative approach. Frankly, it can be. The act of mirroring is, however, a neutral technique. It's the negotiator's intention that can make it manipulative. If you don't intend to use it to quickly establish genuine rapport, you have created nothing to carry forward. The goal of customer negotiation is not only to *get* a customer, but to *keep* that customer. The only way mirroring will support that goal is if you establish genuine rapport. Using mirroring manipulatively is actually acting against your long-term interest in the negotiation because no one likes to be manipulated. It does not establish a foundation for a lasting relationship.

3 Secrets for Success in Customer Negotiation

Showing up and getting in sync will help you listen skillfully. But even when you do listen skillfully, you will likely miss something. To make sure you really do understand the person, check in. The next section of the book will show you how to check in and confirm your understanding.

Confirm Understanding

He that answereth a matter before he heareth it, it is folly.

Proverbs 18:13

Listening is not enough, even when you do it skillfully. You understand someone when you understand what the person *means*, not just what the person says. We need to check in because words mean different things to different people. As we listen, we routinely filter what we hear through our own definitions, agendas, preconceived notions, expectations, experiences and emotions. We assume that because we know what something means to us, it must mean the same thing to everyone. The result is that we don't hear what they mean.

By way of example, let's go back to the hotel where housekeeping wanted new vacuums. A guest at the exclusive and trendy boutique hotel asked the concierge to recommend a "casual" restaurant. The concierge did not inquire into what the guest meant by "casual" and sent the guest to a casual dining restaurant/bar—a chain restaurant. The wealthy and sophisticated guest berated the concierge when he returned to the hotel. He couldn't believe the concierge would send him to "that" kind of restaurant. In the guest's mind, "casual" meant a high-end restaurant where you didn't need to wear a tie! Meaning is in people not in words.

When was the last time you jumped to a conclusion or made an assumption only later to find out that it was wrong? How many times have you said, "Oh, I didn't know that is what you meant." Did

3 Secrets for Success in Customer Negotiation

it wind up costing you time and money to untangle it later? How many sales have you lost because you assumed you understood what the client wanted, but missed the mark? It has been said, "The greatest enemy of communication is the illusion of it."[7] To avoid the illusion of communication, take responsibility to *check in* to see if you really do understand.

How do you check in? Pause, shift, rephrase and reflect.

Pause and Shift

Conversation is a lot like driving a high-performance sports car: to achieve maximum performance—to really see what that baby can do—you first have to pause and shift. Imagine that you are driving a Porsche; a red one with tan interior. Unlike a car with an automatic transmission, the Porsche requires you to ease your foot off the gas, push down on the clutch to disengage the gears, shift gears, ease off the clutch and then put on the gas. If your red

Porsche has six gears, you have to do it six times to get to maximum speed! It's another paradox. You can't reach maximum performance by keeping your foot on the gas. Conversations are just like driving that Porsche: in conversations you periodically have to pause—metaphorically engage the clutch—and shift your attention to understand what the speaker means. You need to pause and check your understanding before you respond to the speaker.

> **Key point:** Pause and check your understanding before you respond!

You can pause and check your understanding by a simple active listening process: rephrasing and reflecting. Rephrasing addresses the verbal aspect of communication and reflecting addresses the non-verbal aspect. Let's look at each part of the rephrasing and reflecting process.

Rephrasing: Check in to Confirm What Is Said

To rephrase, simply restate in your own words (summarize or paraphrase) what you think someone is saying. Wouldn't you feel that someone was making an extra effort to hear you if they said, "Let me see if I understand you," and then paraphrased what they heard you say? Or if they paused and said, "So, is this what you mean?" That's the feeling you want to elicit when you pause in a conversation just long enough to play it back for clarity. Because we all want to be understood, the speaker will want to clarify his or her meaning if you didn't fully understand. Then you are ready to hit the gas and go forward.

Here's the rephrasing process:

1. Allow the speaker to finish.

2. *Pause*—put in the clutch.

3. Summarize what you think you heard.

4. When the speaker confirms that you understand, then reply.

An example of this process—one that you probably use daily—is confirming a telephone number. When someone gives you a telephone number, you pause and repeat it to make sure you got it right. If you didn't the other person will correct you.

When you first start applying rephrasing to conversations other than telephone numbers, it can feel awkward—not unlike driving a stick shift for the first time if you have had that experience. But it's not how smooth you are that is important; it's the intention behind the technique that matters most. If you have a sincere desire to understand the speaker, then your efforts will be well received even if you are not smooth. You may find a lead-in helpful as you start to confirm understanding. For instance, you might say, "If I understand you, _____." Fill in the blank by rephrasing what you understood in your own words. You will eventually get into a natural listening sequence that includes listen, pause, confirm your understanding and then respond.

Reflect: Check in to Understand Emotions

The active listening process of rephrasing or paraphrasing is becoming more prevalent. That's understandable because it is a powerful technique for a negotiator. But how do you avoid being misled by what someone *isn't* saying? That requires a more uncommon skill: the ability to communicate back what you are seeing or sensing. Reflecting is about checking in to confirm what is going on at the emotional level of the negotiation. Emotions can be powerful drivers in a negotiation. Our emotions are expressed in our body language. Only a small fraction of what is communicated between people is transmitted by words alone. The rest is transmitted by non-verbal communication—facial expression, gestures, tone of voice and movement.

You can sense (see, hear or feel) when someone is frustrated, concerned or happy. Many—I believe most—negotiators avoid dealing with these emotions. They see them; they just don't talk about them. It's like the Hans Christian Andersen fairy tale about the emperor's new clothes. All the villagers admire the naked emperor as he parades through the town in his magic clothes. They are afraid to believe their own eyes but don't speak up until a child says, "Where are the emperor's clothes?" It is important to speak up about emotions during a negotiation—to get them on the table. Lurking, but unaddressed, negative emotions can crater negotiations and destroy customer relationships.

Let's say that the person with whom you are negotiating seems frustrated to you about a requirement. Reflect what you are sensing. You might say, "You (appear, sound or seem) frustrated." That opens the door to a discussion about how the other person is actually feeling. It makes emotions explicit rather than implicit. You may find that the person is not frustrated—I often find I get it wrong. Regardless of whether I have pegged the emotion correctly, my experience is that the person will clarify how they are actually feeling. The person, for instance, might clarify, "I'm not really frustrated, I'm concerned about whether we can satisfy that requirement." What appeared to be frustration turned out to be concern. Again, we all want to be understood. A person's natural instinct is to clarify any misunderstanding if you are making a sincere effort to understand how the person is feeling.

By the way, reflecting does not only apply to negative emotions. It can also be helpful to reflect positive emotions. For instance, "You seem happy about this approach."

Here's the reflecting process:

1. Allow the speaker to finish

2. *Pause*—put in the clutch.

3. Summarize what you think you see or sense—emotions.

4. When the speaker confirms that you understand, then reply.

I have found that putting my perception of a customer's emotions on the table can have four benefits:

First, it allows customers to fully express themselves.

Second, in the process of expressing themselves, customers often gain clarity about how they actually feel.

Third, we both proceed with greater understanding about what is going on at the emotional level of the negotiation.

Fourth, there is an opportunity to let off steam. If a customer is feeling frustration or anger, the opportunity to vent creates a more constructive environment as we move forward.

In the next section, Manage Reactions, you will see how reflecting can be used as an effective technique to avoid being taken in by a very common negotiation tactic.

> **Key point:** There is a simple process for checking your understanding. Pause and Rephrase (summarize or paraphrase) what you heard the speaker say or Reflect emotions (what you see or sense).

Manage Reactions

Unfortunately, a common negotiation ploy is to provoke reaction. When the other party gets you to react, you lose balance and stop thinking coolly. You move from your power zone—your ability to think calmly—and power shifts to the other party. You may find the other party in the negotiation is attacking your proposal, or even you. The tactic is to attack (press, pressure, hassle, rant, rage, insult, take an extreme position) until they provoke a reaction from you.

Both Sides Win

If you encounter this ploy, don't react; keep your cool. Don't return in kind. How do you keep your cool? Pause, shift and get curious. Put the emotions around the attack on the table by using the reflecting process. For instance, "You clearly seem angry with me." Rather than giving up power, you are exercising your power as a negotiator to get curious. You are constructively addressing a clear barrier to a productive negotiation by reflecting what you are seeing or sensing rather than reacting. If it is a ploy, you have likely just gotten the other party off balance because you are not reacting the way you were expected to react. By contrast, if there is a substantive problem provoking the reaction, you will surface it so you can deal with it. Either way, you are positioning yourself to benefit.

Nance Guilmartin says it succinctly in her Power of Pause Practice #6: "Get curious, not furious."[8] Guilmartin advances this practice as a response to "emotional highjacking"—a term introduced by Daniel Goleman in his book *Emotional Intelligence*. Guilmartin

3 Secrets for Success in Customer Negotiation

describes "emotional highjacking" this way: "That's when our biology overpowers reason and triggers an emotional response set off by nothing more than a word, a tone of voice, a look, or even a memory."[9] Unprincipled negotiators try to enhance their power by triggering an emotional response. Although I view an intention to win in a negotiation through emotional highjacking as unprincipled, it can unfortunately be effective. Hardball negotiation is an example of an effort at emotional highjacking.

You need to manage your reactions when faced with hardball negotiators. You often encounter hardball negotiators with customers who try to capitalize on their power as a buyer to hammer you on price. Baseball is a great metaphor for hardball negotiation.

Understand first that the game the customer is playing in hardball negotiation is win-lose negotiation. Like a pitcher, a buyer playing hardball relentlessly pitches the fact that you have competition and therefore you need to lower your price. The buyer wants to make you swing at price to keep the level of the negotiation on price rather than value or what differentiates your product or service. The buyer wants to trigger a defensive reaction where you are defending your price. When those fast balls are coming at you, there are a couple of defensive swings that can strike you out!

The first swing that strikes out is probing. A natural reaction to a hard line on price is to probe for information. You need information if you are going to make a case for value-add or to differentiate your product or service. In hardball negotiation the customer does not want to give you information; cards are held close to the vest. So the tendency is to probe harder. The harder you probe, the more the other party resists giving you information.

Although salespeople are frequently encouraged to probe for information, probing for information is generally only moderately successful. Why? Because people don't like to be probed. In fact, in any kind of negotiation, if your customer doesn't

3 Secrets for Success in Customer Negotiation

believe that answering your question is in his or her best interest, you will get selective information at best. Probing questions generally come up short in any environment because we are not wired as humans to give information that seems to be against our interest. Questions get routed through our brain in such a way that our response is inhibited if, on an unconscious level, we don't sense that answering your question is in our best interest. It's a physiological defense mechanism. A feeling of trust overcomes this defense mechanism.

Trust is the gateway to information; rapport and understanding are the gateways to trust. Your ability to show up and get in sync begins to position you to overcome the unconscious barrier the customer has to giving you information. It is far more effective than launching into probing.

Another swing that strikes out is persuading—launching into your sales pitch. A quick counter to a customer's objections without pausing to check your understanding can feel like a sales pitch. Probably because it is a sales pitch. Most of us like to buy; we just don't like to be sold—even when we are playing hardball. When you immediately start selling me on your position without pausing to understand my objection, you are reacting rather than responding. You are basically telling me that my objection is not valid and here's why. It's good for a courtroom, but not for a customer. Rather than an immediate counter, first confirm your understanding. "So Mr. Customer, if I understand you, you have these objections." You have just invoked the influence principle of reciprocity to aid you. It is harder to sustain my hardball approach when you respond with an effort to understand me; it is easier when you immediately counter with your sales pitch. When the customer confirms that you understand his or her objections, then swing.

Interpretation is a good swing. For instance, you might say, "If you have that objection, I assume you have this type of need or interest." Because we all

3 Secrets for Success in Customer Negotiation

want to be understood, the customer will very likely clarify his or her need or interest if your interpretation is not correct. You have taken the best swing you can to access the information you need to be effective in the negotiation. You've given the best response to a hardball pitch.

Hardball negotiation is an aggressive approach intended to get you off of your game—to create emotional highjacking. So stay on your game. Build on Guilmartin's Power of Pause principle and get curious rather than defensive. The customer can only win if you swing when the customer pitches price and competition. Don't swing. Like in baseball, you can choose when and how to swing! When you manage your reactions, when you pause and get curious rather than react defensively, you invoke *influence in response to power*. You create an opportunity to change the game in your favor.

Key point: Follow Nance Guilmartin's advice and "get curious, not furious."

Both Sides Win

Practice 2: Know Your Value

A T SOME POINT in the negotiation you get around to price, rate or fee—the money. One of the most costly mistakes a negotiator can make is to assume that the lowest price wins. Rarely are decisions made solely on the basis of price. My conversations over the years with master negotiators have confirmed my personal experience that price is the most overestimated aspect of a negotiation. That being said, customers naturally want the best deal they can get. But the *best* deal has more to it than price, rate or fee. The *best* deal is about value. Value is the sum of price and worth. Your value may well be worth more to the customer than the lowest price available. None of us buy products and services; we buy what the product or service does for us—the benefit. Communicating added benefit can create leverage for you to enhance your price. Remember, just because someone is offering a lower price does not mean that it is a *better* price.

To illustrate this point, I'd like to share a story about a banker friend of mine. He is a high-performance bank lender who has a long track record of doing high-return commercial loans. He had banked a local doctor for many years. In addition to his medical practice the doctor owned a hobby farm. When the doctor died, a lender from a competitor bank approached his children with a lower mortgage rate on the farm. The kids told my banker friend that unless he could match the rate, they would have to go with the competitor. Now my banker friend had no intention of competing on rate— he never does. Instead, he did two things.

First, he converted the rate into dollars to make it more understandable. People don't spend or pay rates, they spend or pay dollars. Although the rate differential sounded large when talking percentages, the actual dollar

3 Secrets for Success in Customer Negotiation

value was only several hundred dollars a year to some very wealthy customers. The children were surprised that it was so little. Stating the benefit in terms that the customer can easily understand and quantify is a high-impact negotiation strategy.

Second, he talked about the benefit their father had realized over the years. He reminded them that he had been there with a fair deal during good times and bad—and that there had been bad days for the farm. Did they really want to transfer the loan in view of their history together? The answer turned out to be "no."

There is a tendency to underestimate the value-add of a good relationship—of history together. If you have performed consistently, then there is risk in *not* doing business with you on an ongoing basis. The motivation to avoid risk is often more compelling than an opportunity for gain. Although a competitor may offer a lower price, there is a potential switching cost. Can the competitor really deliver the value that you have delivered over time? Has the competitor put

———— ◆ • ————

enough on the table to compensate the customer for taking the risk of switching? Potential loss of benefit is a compelling dimension of your value with an existing customer.

My banker friend tells me that he gets frustrated because his lenders routinely underestimate the value of their relationships and cave in to a lower rate offered by a competitor. The willingness to cave in may be symptomatic of a failure to truly understand their value.

> **Key point:** A lower price does not mean that it is a *better* price. That being said, customers naturally want the best deal they can get. But the best deal has more to it than price, rate or fee. The *best* deal is about value. Value is the sum of price and worth. Know your value!

3 Secrets for Success in Customer Negotiation

Calculate Your Value Equation

You can't effectively argue for value if you haven't fully defined it in your own mind. The following value equation will help you delineate your value. You are at risk of underestimating your value if you haven't calculated your value equation prior to a negotiation.

Numerator: What the Customer Gets

(Product/Service + Added Benefits)

Denominator: What the Customer Pays

A value equation has both a numerator and a denominator. You will naturally default to the denominator (what the customer pays) if you don't have a clear understanding of the numerator (what the customer gets).

Understanding your added benefits is where you gain leverage in a negotiation. It is important to remember that people don't buy products and services; rather, they buy what the product or service does for them. This point is beautifully illustrated by a question posed by Leo McGinneva: "Why do people buy quarter-inch drill bits?" The answer is: "They don't want quarter-inch bits. They want quarter-inch holes."[10] Let's apply Mr. McGinneva's question to coffee: "Why would people pay $2.14[11] for a tall (small) cup of Starbucks' coffee?" There are certainly much cheaper cups of coffee to be had. When I ask that question in negotiation workshops, Starbucks drinkers have many answers. Although some people prefer the taste, it's clearly not just about the coffee. Others like such things as convenience, consistency, variety, atmosphere and the prestige of the brand (Starbucks is consistently ranked as one of the top 100 most valuable global brands). One participant would only buy from Starbucks because he liked the cup! Starbucks clearly knows its value. As a result, Starbucks has created loyal customers who are willing to pay a premium price for the value they believe they receive.

My experience is that people tend to think too generically about value. For example, someone might include "convenience" as a value-added benefit when defining the numerator of their value equation. "Convenience" is too generic. You will gain from drilling down to make the value more customer-specific. How is your product or service convenient for the customer? Let's say a customer can get to your store 15 minutes faster than they can get to your nearest competitor. Sharing that specific information has far greater impact than merely telling a customer that you are convenient. It is helpful to both quantify and develop proof points for each of the benefits you deliver to a customer.

Doing the math on your value equation tends to enhance your power as a negotiator. You know why a customer should do business with you. You can talk both sides of the value equation: price and worth. Knowledge truly is power. In a negotiation you increase your power when you have knowledge of both the customer's needs and how your benefits satisfy those needs.

BOTH SIDES WIN

———◆———

Key point: Remember, people don't buy quarter-inch drill bits; they are really buying quarter-inch holes! In a negotiation you increase your power when you have knowledge of both the customer's needs and how your benefits satisfy those needs. Define your Value Equation prior to a negotiation.

Practice 3: Understand Your Personal Power

POWER IS THE ABILITY to do something—to achieve an outcome you want. Positional power and personal power are two types of power. Positional power comes from a person's role, position or authority; it's derived from external sources. A customer, by definition, has positional power because the customer is in the position to make the final buying decision. By contrast, personal power is derived internally. Personal power is rooted in things that you control like knowledge, skill, preparation, aspiration and commitment. For instance, understanding and applying communication and influence principles increases personal power in a negotiation. Even when you are faced with someone who has greater positional power than you have, you can, nonetheless, influence the outcome by leveraging sources of personal power. Unfortunately, many—maybe most—negotiators either fail to recognize their sources of personal power or act in ways that give their power away. Knowing your value (Practice 2) is an example of a source of personal power. Not knowing your value is one way to give away power in a negotiation. You can't effectively argue for value if you haven't first fully defined it in your own mind. Some other inherent sources of personal power that negotiators either fail to recognize or tend to give away include:

Having a high aspiration level.

Having a clear walk-away position.

Being prepared.

3 Secrets for Success in Customer Negotiation

Let's take a look at each of these sources of personal power together with ways that negotiators routinely give that power away.

> **Key point:** Understand and capitalize on your sources of personal power.

Personal Power Source: High Aspiration Level

Your "aspiration level" is your expectation of the likely outcome of the negotiation—what you want to achieve. I have been interested over the years in social research that draws the connection between aspiration level and the outcomes achieved in a negotiation. Bottom line: research is consistent with my own experience that negotiators with higher aspirations tend to achieve better results. We don't typically achieve outcomes beyond the level of our aspirations; so aspirations can often be a form of self-limiting belief. When helping people prepare for a negotiation, I get curious about their aspiration level. I routinely ask three questions:

1. What do you need?

2. What do you want?

3. What would be an extraordinary outcome?

People can generally respond reasonably well to questions 1 and 2—they are reasonably clear about what they need and want from a negotiation. The answer to question 3—what would be extraordinary— is a different matter. After some prodding a person will give me an answer to question 3, but it is almost always given with a caveat about why it can't be achieved. "Well this would be extraordinary, *but* he won't agree to that." There is a pervasive tendency to argue against the extraordinary! That's why aspiration levels can be self-limiting beliefs. When asking someone to aim high, a pesky little "yeah but" usually wants to creep in.

3 Secrets for Success in Customer Negotiation

In reality, however, you will often find that the "yeah buts" lack substance; that extraordinary outcomes are often more possible than one might think.

I got a lesson about the possibility of the extraordinary many years ago during a negotiation for a new car. At the time, I was young in my marriage and in my career—I was a young lawyer with a very high opinion of my negotiating skills. I was not, however, familiar with the power of aspiration. A lesson was forthcoming.

The car we selected had a base model and two option packages. Although I really wanted both option packages, the auspices of financial prudence dictated that we buy only one. So I concluded the negotiation, and we bought the car with fewer options. As my wife and I were walking out of the salesman's office, she said, "I think we should have bought the fully-loaded model." I was gung ho until she said, "At the same price." Then came the "yeah but." I reminded her that I had just exercised my prodigious negotiation skills and that we had bought the model that was not fully-loaded.

She said, "Just ask him." I swallowed my pride—not an easy task—and asked him. He said, "Are you serious?" I said, "Apparently, I am." With some persistence on my part, the salesman asked the owner of the dealership to sell us the fully-loaded model for the price we had just negotiated for the lesser model. To both the salesman's and my surprise, he said, "OK." We ended up with the fully-loaded model for the same price that I had negotiated for the model with fewer options!

Needless to say—after my wife trained me—I have negotiated very beneficial car deals over the years. However, I apply what I learned about aspiration levels to all negotiations. I've trained myself to go into a negotiation with a high aspiration level. I ask myself, "What would be extraordinary?" That question tunes me into a source of personal power.

You give away that personal power by going into a negotiation with too low an aspiration level. Aim high and push through the "yeah buts." When you ask yourself what would be an extraordinary outcome, your

3 Secrets for Success in Customer Negotiation

first instinct might be, "Yeah, that would be great, but he will never do that." You may be right; but then again, you may be wrong. You don't know until you explore it during the negotiation. Some of my favorite calls are the ones from clients telling me that they have just negotiated an extraordinary outcome. I can assure you of one thing: your chances of achieving an extraordinary outcome are limited if you don't first aspire to achieve the extraordinary. Again, I encourage you to aim high and push through those limiting "yeah buts."

> **Key point:** Aim high: ask yourself what would be an extraordinary outcome? Then push through the limiting "yeah buts."

In my experience, not only do negotiators tend to have too low an aspiration level, they compound it by having too high an estimation of a customer's alternatives. In a customer negotiation the alternative generally has a name: the competition. Don't let your estimate—which is likely a guesstimate—of the strength of the competition limit your aspiration level.

It is helpful to remember that you are not competing with your competition: you are competing with your customer's *perception* of your competition. Your customer is not viewing the competition objectively. Competition is in the mind of the customer. If you are concerned about a competitor, or the customer brings up a competitor, an effective negotiation strategy can be to simply get curious about what the customer likes about the competitor's value proposition. You may find that the customer does not value the competitor nearly as much as you think or for the reasons that you think. That was the case with a client of mine who was developing a sales proposal for a very large deal with a prospective customer; let's call the prospective customer "Newco."

My client knew that there was a competitor that was currently doing business with Newco and that had been doing business with Newco for a number of years. My client also knew that there was a strong personal relationship between Newco and one of the senior executives of the competitor. The competitor has a history of very aggressive pricing. My client was pricing their proposal based on their *perception* of the price competitiveness of the incumbent. Several members of the sales team were arguing for going in very low to compete against the incumbent competitor. Their perception was that the competitor had a leg up because the competitor was currently doing business with Newco and had a personal relationship; they had to go in low to displace the competitor. Before adopting the "go in low" strategy, however, I encouraged my client to get curious with Newco about the competitor. A very pleasant surprise awaited them.

When my client asked Newco what Newco valued about the competitor's services, they were surprised to find out that the competitor was not being considered for future work. Although Newco liked the competitor and they had a long-standing relationship, the competitor could not provide all of the services that Newco needed; my client could. Newco needed a sole-source supplier for all of their needs. With that knowledge, my client's price aspirations increased substantially. They were able to do a deal that was mutually beneficial to both parties and fully compensated them for the value they now provide Newco as a sole-source supplier.

You don't always get what you ask for; but you never get what you don't ask for. In customer negotiation there can even be value in not getting what you ask for. If the customer isn't willing to share thoughts about the competition, that, in itself, is important knowledge. It tells you that the customer is still guarded. As noted earlier, questions get routed through our brain in such a way that our response is inhibited if, on an unconscious level, we don't sense that answering your question is in our best interest. It's a defense mechanism. It puts me on alert if a prospective customer won't share with me what they value about a competitor. If they feel too vulnerable to share that information, I begin to question in my own mind whether the competitor is really that strong an alternative for the customer.

You don't generally have to ask about the competition if they are offering a lower price—customers like to volunteer that information. Remember, a lower price is not necessarily a *better* price. Get curious about the value proposition that is associated with the price. You may discover that the price comparison is really a comparison of apples to oranges because you offer more value for your price.

Key point: Competition is in the mind of the customer. Check your assumptions. If you are concerned about a competitor, or the customer brings up a competitor, an effective negotiation strategy can be to simply get curious about what the customer likes about a competitor's value proposition. You may find that the customer does not value the competitor nearly as much as you assumed.

Personal Power Source:
Clear Walk-away Position

At some point, *no deal* may be your best alternative. Knowing when to walk away is a source of personal power in a negotiation.

Never underestimate the power of knowing what you will do if you *can't* negotiate an acceptable outcome. If you don't know your bottom line you may become unsure or tentative if things aren't going your way. Having a bottom line makes it easier to stand up to pressure and temptations. Making a deal that is against your best interests is not a good deal, though it often happens. Then the rationalization starts: "We gave in on that, but it will help build the relationship in the long run." The only thing it generally does for the relationship is demonstrate that you will act in the customer's interest against your own. That does not build a relationship that supports mutual gain.

3 Secrets for Success in Customer Negotiation

A common negotiation tactic involves the dynamic of eleventh-hour crunch time. The tactic plays on our common reaction to deadlines. There is a tendency to feel pressure to make concessions as a deadline approaches. Indeed, most concessions in a negotiation are made at the last minute or in the eleventh hour. We tend to resist walking away after we have invested a lot of time and energy—and perhaps money—in a negotiation. The crunch-time tactic is to make unexpected demands at the eleventh hour. The assumption is that you are too invested in the deal by that time to walk away.

The better you manage yourself during the last few days, hours or minutes of a negotiation, the better the outcome you will achieve. A key to managing yourself effectively during crunch time is to know your walk-away position.

A group that I was negotiating with tried this tactic on us. An energy company that I worked for asked me to negotiate the sale of one of our business units. The business unit we were selling had old pipeline assets. Some of the pipelines had been put in the ground in the 1930s, and there was very little engineering data. We hadn't had any environmental problems and didn't think there were environmental problems, but we just didn't have enough information to know with certainty. My company was clear that it wanted to get completely out of the business and didn't want any lingering liability that would need to be addressed in any future sale of the larger company. Our bottom line: if we couldn't find a buyer who would assume the ongoing environmental liability, we would just stay in the business until we sold the larger company.

When we started negotiating with a prospective buyer, we were very clear up front that we would not give an environmental warranty. We explained why. The other party agreed and we proceeded with a lengthy negotiation.

On the morning of the closing, an environmental warranty appeared in the final closing documents. We explained that we would walk away from the deal if it was not removed. The other side said they couldn't believe we would walk away from the deal over a warranty. As we got up from the table and walked through the door, they discovered otherwise. We didn't cave to the crunch-time pressure. They caught us at the elevator and agreed to remove the warranty. We closed.

The tactic backfired on them: they had to assume the liability and they left money on the table. Had they negotiated the warranty up front—gotten curious about our interests—they may have discovered that we were prepared to make price concessions to persuade the other party to assume the liability. By waiting until the eleventh hour and using a crunch-time pressure tactic, they came up short. We knew our bottom line and were prepared to stick to it. It was a source of personal power for us.

Key point: Most concessions in a negotiation are made at the last minute or in the eleventh hour. We tend to resist walking away after we have invested a lot of time and energy—and perhaps money—in a negotiation. The crunch-time tactic is to make unexpected demands at the eleventh hour because it is assumed you are too invested to walk away. You likely won't walk away if you don't have a walk-away position. Know your bottom line and be prepared to stick to it. It is a source of personal power.

Personal Power Source: Being Prepared

Famed Spanish writer Miguel De Cervantes observed that: "To be prepared is half the victory." Negotiators who think that they can "shoot from the hip" or "wing it" generally fail to capitalize on their full personal power. Opportunity favors the mind that is prepared because you see opportunity you might otherwise overlook and you are better able to manage reactions.

It is true that most of our days are plagued with strong time limitations. I have found, however, that I improve my success by pausing before a negotiation to focus on the following four areas: my goal, my commitment, their goal and the relationship. Let's briefly consider each area of focus.

Your Goal

When defining your goal it is also valuable to get clear on *why* you want to achieve the goal. By considering why the outcome is important to you, you help clarify your own underlying needs and interests.

Then follow Chef Emeril Lagasse's counsel and "take it up a notch!" What would be an extraordinary outcome for you?

Finally, define your walk-away position. Your

walk-away position is really about alternatives. If you have a better alternative to the deal that's on the table, it makes sense to walk away. If you don't know if you have a better alternative, it is hard to walk away. So the key is to consider your alternatives—before you start negotiating.

Your Commitment

The poet John Beecher observed that: "Strength is a matter of the made-up mind." By being clear with yourself about your commitment, you are making up your mind on *how* you plan to negotiate.

- Are you committed to getting curious about underlying needs and interests—theirs and yours?

- Are you committed to listening effectively and building sincere rapport?

- Are you committed to preserving and

exercising your sources of personal power?

The distinction I'm making is between being committed to an outcome and being committed to the practices that will drive that outcome. The three practices we have explored in this book are drivers of successful outcomes in a negotiation. By being genuinely committed to mastering and using these practices, you will take actions to achieve your goals.

Their Goal

Spend some time before you negotiate imagining what it might be like to walk in the other party's shoes. What are their needs and interests? What are their alternatives? Are there possible reasons that their alternatives might not be as attractive as you think? What I'm encouraging you to do is to "get curious" *before* the negotiation.

What you are really doing while you're

walking around in their shoes is creating a diagnostic framework for your negotiation. You are forcing yourself to think of possible issues and the likely reasons to explain the issues. You will be prepared to explore your conclusions during the negotiation to see if your conclusions are right or wrong. Bottom line: you have better questions!

It is always helpful to remember that you don't negotiate with a company; you negotiate with a person. So consider the goal of the individual you are negotiating with as well as the goal of the enterprise on whose behalf the individual is negotiating.

The Relationship

In order to build a relationship as you negotiate, you have to keep reason and emotion in balance—theirs and *yours*. You are better able to maintain balance if you have given some advance thought to the emotional side of the negotiation.

3 Secrets for Success in Customer Negotiation

In Practice 1 we discussed approaches on how to manage reactions during a negotiation. It is important to remember that it is not only the other party's difficult behavior that you need to manage in a negotiation; you also have to manage your own behavior. A natural tendency of human beings is to react—to act without thinking—when we are confronted with a difficult situation. How do you react when you encounter a "no" or meet with resistance? Do you argue, strike back or break off? Although these are very common reactions, they don't promote a good relationship.

As human beings, we have the remarkable—and perhaps unique—ability to think about our own thoughts. This ability to become aware of ourselves enables us to plan for the future, imagine the thoughts of others and project our experiences. We can think about how we might react before we react. Self-awareness provides us with the unique ability to control ourselves intentionally by imagining ourselves in a situation we might encounter in the future and talking to ourselves about options for handling those situations productively.

Self-awareness is a key to self-control and self-control is another source of personal power. In preparation for a negotiation:

> *Ask yourself:* How might I react if I get a "no" or if I get pushback? Is there anything else the other party could do that would trigger a reaction in me?

> *Ask yourself:* What could I do to maintain my self-control in the face of those potentially triggering behaviors by the other party?

The problem is not that you have the emotions; the important part for developing the relationship is how appropriately you express the emotions. You are better able to express emotions appropriately if you have given some advance thought to the emotional side of the negotiation.

3 Secrets for Success in Customer Negotiation

Key point: In preparing for a negotiation, it is helpful to focus on the following four areas: my goal, my commitment, their goal and the relationship. *My goal:* When defining your goal, get clear on *why* you want to achieve the goal. By considering why the outcome is important to you, you help clarify your own underlying needs and interests. *My commitment:* By being clear with yourself about your commitment, you are making up your mind on *how* you plan to negotiate. Commit to the practices that will drive the outcomes that you want. *Their goal:* Consider the goal of the individual you are negotiating with as well as the goal of the enterprise on whose behalf the individual is negotiating. *The relationship:* Self-awareness is a key to self-control and self-control is source of

———◆———

personal power that builds relationships.
Ask yourself: What could I do to maintain
my self-control in the face of potentially
triggering behaviors by the other party?

Final Words

I FIND CUSTOMER negotiation to be the most rewarding kind of negotiation because—when you do it well—you create a mutually profitable relationship. And isn't that the essence of business?

I have shared with you three practices that have been secrets for success for me over the years in negotiating great return and great relationship at the same time:

1. Get curious,

2. Know your value and

3. Understand your power and theirs.

I hope these become your secrets for success as you negotiate with your customers—and in all negotiations.

As with any endeavor, doing it well—gaining mastery—takes commitment and practice. The results you can achieve make it worth the effort.

Mastering the discipline to pause and "get curious" is so important to success in negotiation because problems truly seldom exist on the level at which they are expressed. Getting curious about underlying needs and interests expands the pie, surfaces latent opportunities and helps avoid unnecessary compromise and conflict. If you get curious, you will likely avoid the pitfalls of premature problem-solving and the limits of negotiating at the level of positions.

One of the most significant insights I have gained in life is that being understood is vital to all of us. Mastering the ability to show up, get in sync and check understanding by rephrasing and reflecting is not only an essential negotiation competency, it is a life competency. By making the sincere effort to understand someone, you are laying the foundation for trust and influence. If you want someone to listen to you and understand where you are coming from, leverage the power of the influence principle of reciprocity: first listen and understand them and they will naturally be prone to listen and understand you.

You always have sources of personal power in a negotiation. Personal power is rooted in things that you control like knowledge, skill, preparation, aspiration and commitment. You increase your personal power by understanding and applying communication and influence principles. Even when you are faced with someone who has greater positional power than you have, you can, nonetheless, influence the outcome by leveraging sources of personal power. To capitalize on your sources of personal power:

- Know your value. Work the value equation prior to a negotiation.

- Raise your aspiration level. Ask yourself: what would be extraordinary? Then push through the "yea-buts."

- Know when to walk away.

- Prepare.

Self-awareness is a key to self-control, and self-control is a fundamental source of personal power. It is because self-control is a source of personal power that some negotiators will try to diminish it by getting you to react. The assumption is that human beings are prone to reaction—we're reaction machines that can easily be triggered. In reality, we have the remarkable—and perhaps unique—ability to think about our own thoughts. This ability to become aware of ourselves enables us to plan for the future, imagine the thoughts of others and project our experiences. We can think about how we might react before we react. Self-awareness provides us with the unique ability to control ourselves intentionally by imagining ourselves in a situation we might encounter in the future and talking to ourselves about options for productively handling those situations that might trigger us. We also have the ability to confront reaction with curiosity.

3 Secrets for Success in Customer Negotiation

In the final analysis, negotiation is an art because it is a human process. People are human—unpredictable, irrational, uncertain and often frustrating. Negotiation is the back-and-forth communication we use as human beings to wade through the unpredictable, irrational, uncertain and frustrating to get to a place of understanding and agreement. Done well, *both sides win*!

Both Sides Win

Endnotes

1. Guilmartin, Nance, *The Power of Pause, How to Be More Effective in a Demanding, 24/7 World*, Jossey-Bass, 2010.

2. Twain, Mark, *A Connecticut Yankee in King Arthur's Court*, Harper & Brothers, New York, 1899, p. 65.

3. Cialdini, Robert, *Influence Science and Practice*, Allyn and Bacon, Fourth Edition, 2001.

4. Cialdini, p. 20.

5. Cialdini, p. 21.

6. Photograph © Benjamin Devey, 2012, used with permission of the photographer.

7. The quote has been attributed to Pierre Martineau.

8. Guilmartin, p. 79.

9. Guilmartin, p. 57.

10. Levitt, Theodore, *The Marketing Imagination*, The Free Press, 1986. McGinneva is quoted on p. 128.

11. $2.14 was the price of a tall cup of Starbucks' coffee in New Orleans, Louisiana on October 4, 2011.

About the Author

Logan Loomis is a negotiation expert. Thirty years of business, legal and sales experience have given him the opportunity to negotiate business deals, purchases, sales, mergers and acquisitions, commercial contracts, labor contracts and settlements of disputes. His favorite kind of negotiation is customer negotiation where you have to negotiate great return and great relationship at the same time. Logan's workshops on customer negotiation have been delivered to hundreds of participants.

Logan is currently a business consultant helping companies improve sales results and align their business strategies with their talent strategies. He began his career as a corporate lawyer for a prominent

New Orleans law firm. He moved into private enterprise after a decade practicing law. He led sales and marketing efforts as Vice President of Sales and Marketing for LEDCO, Inc., an intrastate natural gas pipeline and natural gas marketing company. He was CEO of Nortech Energy Corp., a natural gas trading and marketing joint venture of a large diversified energy company.

Logan is the author of *Getting the People Equation Right: How to Get the Right People in the Right Jobs and Keep Them*. He holds a BA degree from the University of Texas, Austin and a Juris Doctor degree from Southern Methodist University.